WHAT HUMAN TRAFFICKERS DON'T WANT YOU TO KNOW

A Teen's Guide to Outsmarting Predators

By Lisa N. Williams, MSW

© Copyright Page

What Human Traffickers Don't Want You to Know: A Teen's Guide to Outsmarting Predators

© 2025 by Lisa N. Williams, MSW

For permission requests, please contact:

✉ LisaWms314@gmail.com

ISBN: 979-8-9994997-0-7

Publisher: *Safety & Respect Publishing*

St. Louis, Missouri, USA

Printed in the United States of America. First Edition, 2025

Safety & Respect Publishing
Empowering Pages… Empowering Young Minds One Page at a Time

Contents

DEDICATION

For every teen who was told to stay silent.

For every survivor who was blamed, ignored, or misunderstood.

For the kids I've worked with, the ones I've cried for, and the ones who still don't have the words.

This is for you; You deserve truth, safety, and the power to rise.

CHAPTER 1: WHY THIS BOOK EXISTS

(Journal Prompts, Case File & Action Tools)

FEAR FACTOR BOX:

> **Every 2 minutes,** a teen is approached online by someone with **dangerous intentions.**
>
> Some are groomers.
>
> Some are predators.
>
> Some are traffickers.
>
> Most don't look scary. They look like:
>
> - Friends
> - Followers
> - Flirty strangers
>
> **What they don't want you to know** is that you're being studied, not complimented.

U.S. HUMAN TRAFFICKING STATISTICS (2024)

Estimated Victims: Approximately 24,000 individuals fell victim to human trafficking within the United States in 2024.

Demographics:

Gender: About 75% of identified victims were female.

Age: Approximately 40% of victims were minors.

Prosecutions: The number of persons prosecuted for human trafficking more than doubled from 2012 to 2022, increasing from 805 to 1,656.

Convictions: The number of persons convicted of a human trafficking offense increased from 578 in 2012 to 1,118 in 2022.

WHY THIS BOOK?

Because you're smart. Because you're online.

Because you've seen red flags and second-guessed them.

Because this could happen to someone **you** know. Or even... to **you.**

This book exists because of **awareness** and **protection**. It's not about scaring you. It's about **arming you.**

You can't fight what you don't understand, and traffickers want you to misunderstand them.

WHO THIS BOOK IS MEANT FOR?

- Teens who want to stay sharp
- Teens who think "this would never happen to me"
- Teens who've already had close calls
- Teens who've been targeted, trapped, or tricked, and need to know they're not alone

This book is also for ones who feel ashamed... and don't know how to start talking about it.

CASE FILE: "He Followed Me for Weeks Before I Knew What He Was Doing"

"I met him through a mutual follower. He'd like my posts and comment funny things. After a week he was sending messages to my DM daily. At first, I was like, cool, someone gets me. But then he started asking things. Like, 'You ever feel like your family doesn't see you?' or 'You've got the kind of look that should be seen.'

I just thought he liked me. But looking back? Every question he asked was fishing for *pain*. He was finding the cracks in my life, so he could crawl in.

WHY TRAFFICKERS WIN (Right Now)

Because they don't wait in alleyways.

They slide into DMs. They show up in discord.

They flirt in Snapchat filters.

They give compliments with hidden hooks.

Traffickers are **calculated manipulators**, not just creepy strangers. They win when:

- You're lonely
- You want to feel seen
- You crave attention or validation
- You think no one understands
- You've got secrets you think no one else has

WHAT A COUNSELOR WOULD SAY:

"Teens are supposed to want connection. That's developmentally normal. But predators twist connection into control, and they do it gradually. This book gives you language for what's happening, so you can stop it before it starts... or speak up if you're already caught up in it."

WHAT THIS BOOK WILL TEACH YOU:

- What human trafficking actually looks like
- How traffickers find, study, and recruit teens
- The tricks and traps used in grooming
- How social media is weaponized
- The myths that keep teens quiet and ashamed
- The power of your voice, boundaries, and instincts
- What to say to a friend who's in too deep
- How to spot, block, and report predators

ACTION TOOLS:

- Google "online grooming news stories teens" — and read what real survivors have said
- Make a list of apps you use and highlight the ones where you've received sketchy messages
- Think of a time your gut said "NO" but you ignored it. What happened next?

REAL TALK REFLECTION: Journal Prompts

1. What red flag moments have I already seen, but brushed off?

....

....

2. Do I know someone who has changed suddenly, isolated themselves, or been secretive about a new "friend"?

....

....

3. Why might I hesitate to speak up if something felt wrong online?

....

....

AFFIRMATION

I don't need to wait until it gets dangerous to trust my instincts.

I deserve to be seen, safe, and respected.

I can outsmart anyone who tries to use confusion as a weapon. I will not

be silence-shamed.

CHAPTER 2: MYTHS THAT GET TEENS TRAPPED

(Case File, Tools, Reflection & Affirmation)

FEAR FACTOR BOX:

> Traffickers don't need chains or cages; they use beliefs to keep you stuck.
>
> If they can convince you:
>
> - "This isn't trafficking."
> - "They love me."
> - "I chose this."
>
> …then they don't need to trap your body. They've already trapped your mind.

THE LIES THAT KEEP TEENS VULNERABLE

Traffickers thrive when you:

- Think it only happens to "certain kinds of people"
- Believe "you'd never fall for that"
- Confuse *loyalty* with *manipulation*

Here are the top myths that predators use, and what's actually true.

MYTH #1: "trafficking means getting kidnapped."

Truth: Most traffickers don't snatch teens; they **pull them in slowly**, using attention, gifts, promises, or love.

90% of trafficking cases begin with grooming and not abduction.

MYTH #2: "That only happens in big cities or poor neighborhoods."
Truth: It happens everywhere, in suburbs, small towns, online games, and even in private schools. Predators don't care where you live. They care if you're reachable and isolated.

MYTH #3: "If I agreed to it, it's not trafficking."
Truth: If someone tricked, pressured, or manipulated you, it's exploitation. Consent is not real when fear, grooming, or threats are involved.

MYTH #4: "Only girls get trafficked."
Truth: Boys, LGBTQ+ youth, and nonbinary teens are targeted too — especially if they're isolated, unsupported, or homeless.
Shame and silence are tools traffickers count on.

MYTH #5: "Trafficking always looks violent."
Truth: Most victims are **trauma-bonded;** they don't even realize they're being trafficked at first.
It often looks like:

- A "relationship"
- A job offers
- A way out of a bad home

MYTH #6: "I'd never be that stupid."

Truth: This isn't about intelligence, it's about **vulnerability and manipulation.**

Even the smartest people can fall for predators. That doesn't make them weak, it makes them human.

CASE FILE: "I Thought I Had a Sugar Daddy"

"I saw girls on TikTok talking about getting paid for talking to older guys. I thought, okay, as long as it's not physical. But then he kept pushing. First, it was video chats. Then it was 'just one pic.' Then it was threats.

I didn't feel trafficked. I felt tricked. And by the time I realized it, I was scared to tell anyone."

WHAT A COUNSELOR WOULD SAY:

"Shame is a trafficker's best friend. If you believe it's your fault, you won't get help. The truth is: exploitation often feels like love, help, or attention at first. You're not broken. You're being manipulated."

ACTION TOOLS

Make a list of 3–5 myths you've heard online about trafficking

Talk to a friend: "What would you do if someone offered you money for pics or favors?"

Follow creators who talk about grooming awareness, not just "glow up" culture or #sugardaddy humor

REAL TALK REFLECTION

1. Which myth surprised me the most, and why?

....

...……………………………………………………………….

2. Have I ever believed a lie that kept me silent, ashamed, or confused?

……………………………………………………………...

……………………………………………………………….

3. Why do I think traffickers want teens to believe these myths?

………………………………………………………………..

………………………………………………………………..

AFFIRMATION

I believe the truth, even when it's uncomfortable. I will not let lies lead me into danger.

I'm allowed to be confused but I will not stay confused. I choose clarity, courage, and protection over denial.

CHAPTER 3: HOW GROOMING REALLY WORKS

FEAR FACTOR BOX:

Grooming doesn't start with violence.
It starts with attention.
- Likes on your posts
- "You're different from other people"
- Late-night DMs
- "I'll never leave you"

You think you're in a connection...
but you're actually being trained to obey

WHAT IS GROOMING?

Grooming is when a predator slowly builds trust with you so they can control you later.

It doesn't feel scary at first. It feels like:

- A new friend
- A caring adult
- A dream opportunity
- Someone who finally gets you but behind the kindness... is a trap.

THE GROOMING STAGES (AND HOW THEY WORK)

1. Targeting

The predator looks for someone who seems:

- Lonely
- Rebellious
- Insecure
- Online often
- Without strong adult support

"They liked all my stories for days before they messaged."

2. Gaining Trust

- They say exactly what you want to hear:
- "You're mature for your age."
- "I wish someone treated me like this." "You're not like the others."

They'll listen to your problems but only to use them later.

3, Filling a Need

They figure out what you're missing and offer it:

- "You need money?" – They'll send some.
- "You feel ugly?" – They'll flood you with compliments.
- "You hate home?" – They'll offer escape. But nothing they give is free.

4, Isolation

They slowly cut you off from friends, parents, and teachers.

- "They don't get us."
- "Don't tell anyone — they'll ruin what we have."
- "This is just our secret."

5, Control & Exploitation

Once you're dependent, they flip the script:

- Threats
- Demands
- Shame
- Blackmail
- Physical coercion

You start feeling stuck, like you owe them.

CASE FILE: "He Waited Until I Couldn't Say No"

"We talked for months before anything happened. He made me feel important. He asked about my art, my goals, my bad days.
Then he started pushing, one picture, one favor, one lie at a time.

By the time I realized he was controlling me, I felt like it was too late. I had no one left. And he made sure of that."

WHAT A COUNSELOR WOULD SAY:

"Grooming isn't just about what predators do, it's about how they make victims feel. Loved. Needed. Trapped. Ashamed.
That's why teens don't speak up. It's not fear of danger. It's fear of losing the only person who 'sees them.

GROOMING TACTICS: Red flag list

Tactic	Example Phrase
Fast Flattery	"You're perfect"
Promised Escape	"I can take you away from all this."
Gift-Giving	"Let me get you something nice."
Isolation	"Don't tell anyone, they won't understand."
Emotional Manipulation	"If you loved me, you'd prove it."
Threats	"I'll leak your pics if you tell."

ACTION TOOLS

- Block anyone who demands secrecy
- Write down the first 5 things someone says when they're gaining your trust — look for patterns
- Share the grooming stages with a friend — talk about where you've seen it before
- Never send photos you wouldn't want shown on a school projector, even to "nice" people

REAL TALK REFLECTION

1. Have I ever had someone move too fast, flatter too much, or demand secrets? What did I feel?

....

....

2. Why might I not recognize grooming until it's too late?

....

....

3. Who do I trust that could help me decode red flags before they go
    too far?

....

....

AFFIRMATION

I am not dumb for getting close to someone who hurt me. I am not broken
for needing love.

I will not be controlled by silence, guilt, or threats. I recognize the signs. I
reclaim my story.

CHAPTER 4: THE DIGITAL TRAP

(Tactics, Tools, Reflection & Affirmation)

FEAR FACTOR BOX:

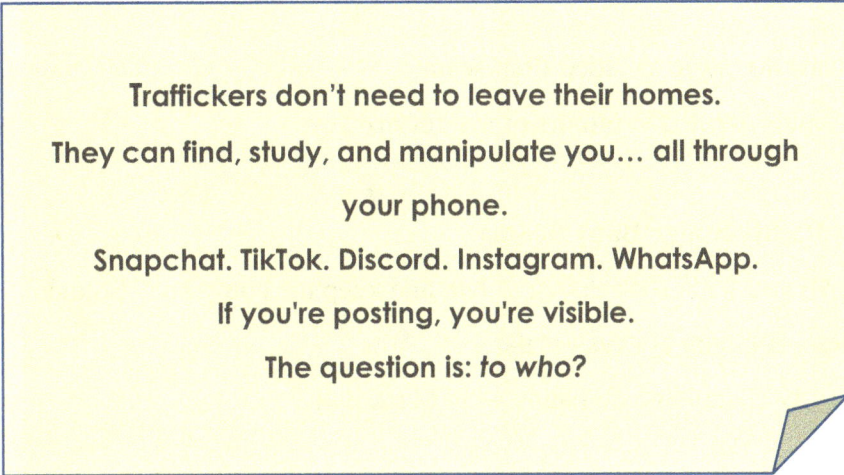

> **Traffickers don't need to leave their homes.**
>
> **They can find, study, and manipulate you... all through your phone.**
>
> **Snapchat. TikTok. Discord. Instagram. WhatsApp.**
>
> **If you're posting, you're visible.**
>
> **The question is: *to who?***

WHY SOCIAL MEDIA IS THE NEW PLAYGROUND FOR PREDATORS

Traffickers use the same apps you do, not to have fun, but to fish for vulnerability. They scroll, they watch, and they wait.

They don't always come in looking scary.

They look like:

- A fan
- A recruiter
- A hot follower
- A "supportive adult"
- A fellow teen who just gets you

THE MOST COMMON DIGITAL TRAPS

"Modeling Agency" or "Talent Scout" DMs

"You have a great look; we're casting for a music video. You'd be perfect."

If they ask for a pic or video first, scam.
Legit scouts don't DM minors or ask for privacy.

Sugar Daddy/Sugar Baby Scams
"I'll give you $500 a week just to talk and keep me company." Sounds harmless. But they always escalate.
From flirty chats → to demands → to blackmail.

"Send me something private" Tricks
"I won't share it. I just want to see more of the real you."
You think you're safe… until they screen record.
Then the threats begin.

Gaming App Grooming
"You're chill. Wanna keep chatting on Snap?"
Discord, Roblox, Fortnite, and even Minecraft have become **predator-friendly spaces** because of voice chat, DMs, and gift trading.

CASE FILE: "He Screen-Recorded Me Without Telling Me"
"We were talking for weeks. He said he was 17, but I never saw his face. He made me feel beautiful. Said he liked girls who were 'real.'

One night I sent something private. Next day, he said he recorded it. He told me to do what he said or he'd send it to my followers.

I felt sick. I was 15.

And now I had no idea how to undo it."

WHAT A COUNSELOR WOULD SAY:

"Sextortion has exploded because it's fast, anonymous, and teens blame themselves. But here's the truth: **you didn't mess up**.

Someone weaponized your trust. You deserve help not shame."

RED FLAGS TO WATCH FOR

Red Flag	Why It's Dangerous
"Let's keep this private."	Isolation = grooming tactic
"Don't tell anyone."	Secret = power imbalance
Fast flattery	Emotional flooding = control
Sketchy job offers	Fake gigs = recruitment front
Anonymous avatars	Hiding identity − predator move
Asking for pics	First ask = first trap

ACTION TOOLS

- A Make your account private and remove followers you don't know in real life

- Use reverse image search (TinEye or Google) on "model scouts" or fake profiles
- Screenshot sketchy DMs before blocking/reporting
- Ask yourself: Would I say this in front of a trusted adult?

REAL TALK REFLECTION

1. Have I ever been asked for something online that made me uncomfortable but I stayed quiet?

....

....

2. What's one post I've shared that revealed more than I realized?

....

....

3. If my younger sibling or cousin got a DM like that — what would I tell them?

....

....

AFFIRMATION

My safety is more important than likes.

I don't owe anyone a reply, a pic, or my privacy. I'm allowed to block, report, and speak up.

I will not let anyone use a screen to silence my power.

CHAPTER 5: WHEN LOVE TURNS INTO LEVERAGE

(Tools, Case File, Reflection & Affirmation)

FEAR FACTOR BOX:

The most dangerous trafficker might not feel like a stranger. They feel like:
- Your boyfriend
- Your ride-or-die
- The one who "gets" you

That's how they win.
They get your heart… before they take your freedom.

WHEN LOVE IS A WEAPON

Traffickers often don't need force; they use affection as bait.

They make you feel:

- Seen
- Chosen
- Important
- Needed
- Loyal

They don't ask for much… at first.

HOW LOVE GETS TWISTED

Love turns into leverage when they start saying things like: "I gave you everything, you owe me this."

"If you leave me, I'll hurt myself."

"We've already come this far; there's no going back."

"No one will believe you anyway."

That's not love. That's emotional control.

CASE FILE: "I Thought He'd Kill Himself if I Left"

"He made me feel like I was all he had. At first, I liked that. It made me feel special. But then he started asking for stuff I wasn't ready for. When I said no, he'd get quiet for days. Or say, 'I guess I'll just disappear.'

One time, he sent a pic of pills.

I stayed. Because I thought not staying would be worse."

WHAT A COUNSELOR WOULD SAY:

"This is called a trauma bond, when someone harms you and makes you feel responsible for keeping them stable.

It's a trap based on fear, not love.

You don't owe someone your body to keep them from falling apart."

SIGNS IT'S LOVE VS LEVERAGE

Healthy Love	Manipulative Leverage
Respects your boundaries	Guilt-trips you for saying no
Encourages you to be yourself	Isolates you from others
Feels calm and safe	Feels tense, rushed, or risky
Listens without pressure	Demands secrets or "proof"
Accepts "no" without punishment	Threatens silence, harm, or breakup

"STAY OR LEAVE?" SCENARIO CHALLENGE

Scenario:

You're dating someone who:

- Asks for passwords "to prove trust"
- Flips out if you talk to certain friends
- Sends you money but expects constant updates
- Once said, "If you leave me, I'll ruin your life."

Would you stay or leave? Why?

....

....

....

REAL TALK REFLECTION

1. Have I ever stayed in something because I felt responsible for the other person's emotions?

....

....

2. How do I know if someone's love is actually healthy?

....

....

3. If my best friend told me these red flags, what would I say to
them?

....

....

ACTION TOOLS

- Write 3 emotional manipulation phrases you've heard or seen, and reframe them with the truth
- Talk to a safe adult about what love vs. loyalty looks like
- Save this phrase: "I'm not responsible for someone else's threats or mental health. I deserve peace and choice."

AFFIRMATION

I don't owe love to people who hurt me.

I can walk away from fear, guilt, and control.

I am not the fixer. I am not the property.

I choose freedom, not fear disguised as love.

CHAPTER 6: WHY TEENS DON'T TELL

(Case File, Tools, Reflection & Affirmation)

FEAR FACTOR BOX:

> **Predators know that if you tell, they lose.**
> **That's why they:**
> - **Threaten you**
> - **Shame you**
> - **Make you feel responsible**
> - **Make you think no one will believe you**
>
> **And too often? They're right.**
> **Because too many teens don't get believed.**
> **But silence is their weapon.**
> **Truth is yours.**

WHY SILENCE FEELS SAFER

Teens don't stay silent because they're weak. They stay silent because:

- "No one would believe me"

- "I'm scared they'll blame me"

- "I don't want to get in trouble"

- "It was kind of my fault, wasn't it?"

- "They said they'd hurt my family"

- "I don't have proof."

- "It's too complicated to explain"

Traffickers count on every one of those thoughts.

CASE FILE: "He Said No One Would Care"

"After everything he did, I still didn't tell. I kept thinking, 'Who's gonna believe me? I followed him. I liked the attention.'

He made me feel like I let it happen. Like I deserved it. So I kept quiet. Even when it hurt. Even when I was scared. Even when I needed help."

WHAT A COUNSELOR WOULD SAY:

"Silence after trauma isn't weakness, it's survival.

When a teen doesn't speak up, it's often because they've been trained not to trust their voice. The truth is: you deserve to be heard. No explanation. No proof. No perfect story."

SHAME LOOP: How Traffickers Use Silence to Stay in Control

- They break your trust
- They make you feel guilty for it
- They convince you to hide it
- You stay silent… and they keep winning

SILENCE vs. SURVIVAL TOOL GRID

Thought	Reframe
"I deserved it."	No one deserves to be used.
"I stayed, so I must've wanted it."	Fear and manipulation are not consent.
"I didn't say no loud enough."	They didn't wait for a yes.
"I can't explain it."	You don't need perfect words to be believed.
"They'll be mad."	You're not responsible for someone else's wrong.

ACTION TOOLS

- Identify 3 people you trust enough to tell if something feels wrong, write them down.
- Practice saying:
- "This is hard to say, but I need to tell you something that made me feel unsafe…"
- Create a private "truth journal", even if you never share it; owning your story is power.

REAL TALK REFLECTION

1. What holds me back from speaking up when something feels off?

....

....

2. Who do I think would believe me — no questions asked?

....

....

3. What would I say to a friend who stayed silent too long?

....

....

AFFIRMATION

I am allowed to speak.

My voice matters, even if it shakes.

I do not have to stay silent for anyone's comfort.

I can ask for help, and I deserve it.

CHAPTER 7: KNOW THE LINGO

How Predators Speak in Code

(Decoder Chart, Case File, Reflection & Tools)

FEAR FACTOR BOX:

Predators don't just watch what you post.

They use emojis, slang, and fake jobs to hide in plain sight. Some teens are being groomed and don't even know it.

Why?

Because the words sound innocent. But the meaning is dangerous

WHY LANGUAGE MATTERS

Traffickers use coded language to:

- Avoid getting caught
- Make exploitation sound "normal"
- Confuse and recruit teens
- Slip through filters, even on protected platforms

PREDATOR CODE: Phrases to Watch Out For

Code Phrase	What It Really Means
"Let me be your mentor."	I want power over you
"Quick cash – no experience needed"	Risky or illegal activity
"Are you down to vibe?"	Looking for a hookup (or worse)
"Pics for points?"	Requesting explicit photos
"Keep it lowkey"	Don't tell anyone, isolation begins
"You got the look for content."	Attempt to sexualize, recruit, or exploit
"Age doesn't matter if we vibe."	Grooming justification
"GFE/BFE available"	Girlfriend/Boyfriend Experience (sex-for-hire slang)
"PPV"	Pay-Per-View (often for explicit content)

EMOJIS TRAFFICKERS USE (Outside Their Normal Context)

Emoji	Hidden Use
🦋🦋	Selling photos or services
🍭🍭	Targeting younger teens (seen as naïve)
🔗🔗	Looking to "trap" or "link up"
💸	Fast money through risky behavior
💧💧🔥🔥	Nudity / sexting request
😈😈	Manipulation, dominance, or sexual intent
🍑	Reference to minors (as in "young/juicy")
🚫🚫⭐	No parental supervision (literally "no cat", no parents)
🎁🎁🎁	Someone being "packaged" or recruited
🚚🚚	Being transported/moved/recruited

CASE FILE: "I Thought It Was Just Flirting"

"This guy kept dropping flame emojis on my stories, then said he could help me get followers. He used all this slang I didn't know, like 'GFE' and 'quick gigs.'

I Googled it.

It was sex work slang.

And I realized... he wasn't flirting. He was recruiting."

WHAT A COUNSELOR WOULD SAY:

"Language is a weapon.

Traffickers use slang to make something dangerous feel casual or even cool. That's why decoding these terms is protection.

If you know what they really mean, you don't get trapped."

ACTION TOOLS

- Screenshot or save this chapter in your notes. Refer to it if something feels off
- Search slang terms you don't understand before responding to DMs
- Follow an Instagram or TikTok account that teaches trafficking and grooming awareness
- Don't assume emojis mean what they look like, ask yourself what context they're being used in

REAL TALK REFLECTION

1. Have I ever heard someone use a phrase or emoji I didn't fully understand, and I went along with it anyway?

....

....

2. If someone I know was being lured with coded slang, how could I help them figure it out?

....

....

3. Why do traffickers prefer coded messages over direct words?

....

....

AFFIRMATION

I will not be confused into silence.

I choose to decode the danger.

I speak the language of truth, not traps.

I'm not naïve, I'm informed and aware

CHAPTER 8: TRAUMA BONDS

Why It's Hard to Walk Away

(Case File, Tools, Reflection & Affirmation)

FEAR FACTOR BOX:

> Some chains don't wrap around your wrists. They wrap around your emotions.
>
> When someone controls you with:
> - Guilt
> - Fear
> - "Love"
> - Rewards and punishments
>
> …that's not a relationship. That's **a trauma bond**. And it's harder to escape than any locked door.

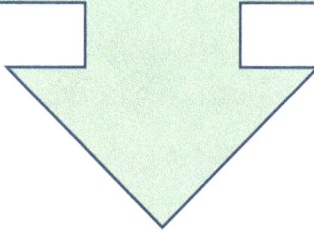

WHAT IS A TRAUMA BOND?

A trauma bond is when you feel emotionally attached to someone who's hurting you. It's not just fear, its confusion, hope, and dependence all mixed together.

You start thinking:

- "They weren't always like this"
- "They're the only one who cares"
- "They need me"
- "It's not that bad"

- "I can't start over"

The more you're hurt… the more you want to fix it.

THE CYCLE OF TRAUMA BONDING

1. Love-bombing: Flattery, gifts, validation
2. Tension building: Guilt, mood shifts, control
3. Abuse or exploitation: Demands, threats, harm
4. Reconciliation: Apologies, tears, promises
5. Calm: Short period of "peace" … before it starts again

You don't realize you're in a trap because every hurt comes with a hug.

CASE FILE: "He Only Hurt Me Because He Loved Me"

"He said I made him crazy. That he got jealous because he cared. He'd scream at me, then cry and say I'm all he has.

I kept saying, 'This isn't abuse. He's just emotional.'

But then I started lying to my friends and hiding bruises and feeling sick when my phone buzzed.

I was scared to stay… and terrified to leave."

WHAT A COUNSELOR WOULD SAY:

"Trauma bonds are strong because your brain is trying to survive, not judge.

When abuse and affection come from the same person, your nervous system stays confused. That's not a weakness. That's trauma.

And you can unlearn it."

SIGNS OF A TRAUMA BOND

If you feel...	You might be trauma-bonded
Fearful of leaving	"I'll ruin everything if I go."
Guilty when they hurt you	"It was probably my fault."
Isolated	"No one else would understand"
Obsessed with fixing them	"If I love harder, it'll stop."
Relieved when they're calm	"See? It's getting better."

ACTION TOOLS

- Write a "Truth List" of 5 ways they've hurt you and don't excuse them
- Ask: "Would I want my best friend in a relationship like this?"
- Practice saying:

"Love shouldn't come with fear. I don't feel safe, and that matters more than feelings."

REAL TALK REFLECTION

1. What's one excuse I've made for someone who treated me badly?

   ....

   ....

2. Do I believe love can exist without pain, guilt, or fear? Why or why not?

   ....

....

3. What support would I need to safely walk away if I ever felt trapped?

....

....

AFFIRMATION

I can love someone and still leave them.

I don't owe loyalty to my pain.

I recognize manipulation, even when it wears a smile.

I am strong enough to break the cycle, and I will

CHAPTER 9: WHAT HAPPENS AFTER YOU LEAVE?

(Recovery Tools, Case File, Reflection & Affirmation)

FEAR FACTOR BOX:

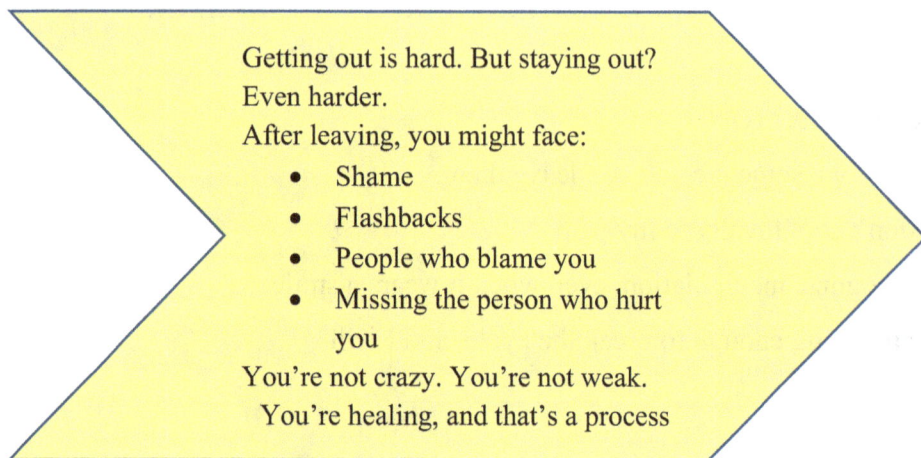

Getting out is hard. But staying out? Even harder.
After leaving, you might face:
- Shame
- Flashbacks
- People who blame you
- Missing the person who hurt you

You're not crazy. You're not weak.
You're healing, and that's a process

WHAT NO ONE TELLS YOU ABOUT AFTERMATH

When teens escape trafficking, grooming, or a toxic bond, they expect to feel free. But instead, many feel:

- Numb
- Confused
- Ashamed
- Angry
- Lonely
- Relieved... but still hurting. Some even go back.

Why?

Because healing isn't a straight line. It's a **cycle of rebuilding what was**

broken.

NORMAL RESPONSES TO TRAUMA

What You Feel	What It Means
Guilt	You've been manipulated into blaming yourself
Numbness	Your body is trying to shut down pain
Nightmares	Your brain is processing threats
Missing them	You were bonded, even if it was toxic
Wanting to go back	Familiar pain can feel safer than unknown freedom

CASE FILE: "I Left… But I Didn't Feel Free"

"When I finally blocked him and walked away, I thought I'd feel proud. But I felt empty.

My friends didn't get it. I couldn't explain. I missed him even though he hurt me. I kept looking at our old messages, like proof I didn't imagine everything.

I thought something was wrong with me. But it was just grief. And healing."

WHAT A COUNSELOR WOULD SAY:

"You don't have to be fully healed to be safe.

Some days, surviving is the victory.

And guess what?

Healing doesn't mean 'getting over it.'

It means learning to live without guilt, fear, and shame dragging you down."

HEALING TOOLS: What You Can Start Doing Now

- Rest without apology – trauma is exhausting
- Journal your real feelings, even if they don't make sense
- Therapy or support groups (in person or online)
- Block the person, even if you're tempted to check in
- Movement – walking, stretching, breathing, dancing
- Talk to someone, even if it's just, "I'm not okay right now"

REAL TALK REFLECTION

1. What am I still carrying that isn't mine to hold?

....

....

2. Who or what makes me feel even 1% safer today?

....

....

3. What would I say to another teen who just walked away from a toxic situation?

....

....

AFFIRMATION

I don't have to rush my healing.

My story is valid, even if it's messy.

I am not what happened to me.

I'm allowed to rest, recover, and rebuild at my pace.

.

CHAPTER 10: WHERE TO GET HELP

Even If You're Scared

(Safe Contacts, Scripts, Tools & Affirmation)

FEAR FACTOR BOX:

> **You might think:**
> - **"If I tell, they'll freak out."**
> - **"They'll call the cops."**
> - **"I'll get blamed."**
> - **"No one will believe me." But silence only protects predators.**
> - **Help is real.**
>
> **It's not always perfect. But it can be safe.**
>
> **And you're allowed to ask, even if your voice shakes**

WHY GETTING HELP FEELS TERRIFYING

For many teens, asking for help feels harder than surviving the abuse. Because help can bring:

- Exposure
- Embarrassment
- Authority figures
- Family drama
- Loss of control

But the truth is: you're still in control when you speak up.

You get to decide:

- Who you talk to

- When you talk

- How much you share

"I DON'T KNOW HOW TO START"

Use these simple scripts:

"I need to tell you something that's hard to say. Please just listen."

"Someone made me feel unsafe, and I don't know what to do."

"I've been keeping a secret because I was scared. But I need help now."

You don't need every detail.

You don't need proof.

You just need your truth.

WHERE TO GET HELP (For Real)

National Resources (U.S.)

Organization	Contact Info	What They Do
National Human Trafficking Hotline	📱 1-888-373-7888 or text "BeFree" to 233733	24/7 help, anonymous, multilingual
National Runaway Safeline	📱 1-800-786-2929 or 1800RUNAWAY.org	Help for teens in crisis or unsafe homes
RAINN (Sexual Assault Support)	📱 1-800-656-4673 or rainn.org	Confidential, 24/7 support & local referrals
Crisis Text Line	📱 Text "HELLO" to 741741	Free emotional support from trained counselors

Who Else Can Help?

- A school counselor, teacher, or coach
- A mentor or youth group leader
- A social worker
- A parent or caregiver you trust
- A friend's parent

- Your doctor or nurse
- A therapist (in person or online)

Even one safe person can change everything.

CASE FILE: "I Told a Teacher, And Everything Changed"

"I was terrified to say it. My voice shook the whole time. I kept expecting her to yell or doubt me. But she didn't.

She sat still. She believed me. She didn't rush me. She helped me get connected to a counselor. And for the first time in months... I didn't feel alone."

ACTION TOOLS

- Make a "Safety Contact List": 3 people you'd consider telling
- Save one of the hotlines in your phone right now
- Practice one of the scripts from this chapter out loud or in writing
- Remind yourself: telling is strength, not betrayal

REAL TALK REFLECTION

1. What's the scariest part about asking for help, and is it 100% true?

   ....

   ....

2. Who has made me feel seen, heard, or safe in the past?

   ....

   ....

3. What would I tell a younger version of myself who felt trapped?

....

....

AFFIRMATION

I am not broken.

I am not dirty.

I am not to blame.

I am worthy of help.

I am allowed to speak.

I am rebuilding.

I survived and now, I rise.

CHAPTER 11: HOW TO HELP A FRIEND IN TROUBLE

What to Say, What Not to Say, and How to Get Real Help

WHY THIS MATTERS

Not everyone who reads this book will be a victim, but everyone knows someone at risk. Maybe it's a friend:

- who started dating an older guy suddenly

- who stopped posting online and became withdrawn

- who seems scared, but won't talk about it

You don't have to be a therapist to help.

You just have to be real, calm, and consistent.

WARNING SIGNS TO WATCH FOR

Your friend might be in danger if:

- They suddenly have gifts/money with no explanation

- They hide their phone or seem secretive

- They're afraid of being alone or don't want to go home

- They're talking to someone way older

- Their personality has changed: withdrawn, anxious, jumpy

- They make weird "jokes" about being controlled, watched, or used

You don't need to confirm everything.

If your gut says "something's off," trust it.

WHAT TO SAY

"I've noticed some stuff that makes me worried. Can we talk?"

"I'm not here to judge you. I just want to make sure you're safe."

"If something's wrong, you don't have to explain everything. You're not alone."

"No one deserves to be scared. I can help you find someone safe to talk to."

WHAT NOT TO SAY

- "Why didn't you just leave?"
- "You're too smart to fall for that."
- "You should've told me sooner."
- "It sounds like you wanted it."
- "Are you serious? That doesn't sound like them…

" Even if you're shocked, stay focused on listening, not fixing.

ACTION TOOLS: HOW TO BE A SAFE FRIEND

Do This	Because...
Stay calm	Panic will shut them down
Listen without interrupting	They've likely never told anyone
Believe them	Even if it sounds unbelievable
Ask how you can support	Not every situation needs the same help

Offer to go with them to a counselor, trusted adult, or call a hotline together.

F YOU NEED TO TELL AN ADULT (And They Say "Don't")

If your friend tells you not to tell anyone, but you know they're in danger, use this script:

"I care about you too much to stay quiet if I think you're in danger. I'll go with you or help you figure out the safest way to get help. But I can't let you go through this alone."

If your friend is being trafficked, hurt, or groomed, telling a safe adult could literally save their life.

SAMPLE TEXTS TO GET AN ADULT INVOLVED

- "Hi. I'm worried about a friend and don't know what to do. Can we talk privately?"

- "Something's going on with a student I know. I'm not sure what, but it feels serious."

- "Can I tell you something that might be uncomfortable, but important?"

AFFIRMATION

I can be a safe space.

I don't have to fix everything to be helpful.

I will speak with care and act with courage.

My voice could help someone survive.

CHAPTER 12: KNOW THE LAW

Teen Edition – What Counts, What's Illegal, and Why It Matters

FEAR FACTOR BOX

> **If it was that serious, someone would've stopped it."**
>
> **That's the trap.**
>
> **Many teens don't realize they're being abused, coerced, or even trafficked because no one ever explained what those words mean.**
>
> **Let's change that**

KNOW YOUR RIGHTS

The law says:

You have the right to be:

- Safe
- Free from coercion (pressure, threats, manipulation)
- Respected, regardless of what you wear, post, or do
- Protected from anyone who uses you for sex, money, or power
- Heard and taken seriously, no matter your age, gender, or background

WHAT COUNTS AS EXPLOITATION?

Exploitation refers to when someone uses you for their gain without your full, informed, and free consent.

This includes:

- Using threats to get sexual or explicit photos
- Offering money, rides, food, or gifts for sex
- Pressuring you to meet someone alone who you met online
- Posting or selling your private images
- Telling you they'll "ruin your life" if you don't do what they say
- Making you recruit other teens

Even if you agreed at first, **coercion cancels consent**.

KEY TERMS TO KNOW

Term	What It Means
Consent	Saying yes freely, without pressure, while fully understanding what you're agreeing to
Coercion	Manipulating someone into doing something they don't really want to do
Grooming	Building trust to later control, exploit, or abuse someone
Human Trafficking	Forcing or tricking someone into sex acts or labor for profit
Child Pornography (CSAM)	Any nude or sexual image of someone under 18, even if they sent it themselves
Mandated Reporter	An adult (like a teacher, coach, or counselor) who is legally required to report abuse

IS THIS ILLEGAL?

Situation	YES or NO
A 22-year-old offering cash to a 16-year-old for "pics"	YES – sexual exploitation of a minor
A teen pressured into sharing nudes by a classmate	YES – coercion & child pornography
A friend gets paid to recruit others to a "modeling gig"	YES – trafficking tactics
A minor agreeing to meet a stranger they met online	Risky, could involve grooming
A teen secretly dating someone 10+ years older	Likely illegal, depending on state laws

CASE FILE: "I Didn't Know It Was a Crime"

"I thought I was just being dramatic.

He didn't hit me. I said 'yes' even though I didn't want to. Then I found out what coercion means, and I cried.

I realized: It wasn't my fault. What he did was a crime.

I just didn't know the words."

ACTION TOOLS

- Learn your state's age of consent laws at www.ageofconsent.net
- If you feel unsure about something, ask: "Would this be legal if I were 10 years older?"
- Report abuse or exploitation anonymously at:

- Report to NCMEC
- Call 1-888-373-7888 or Text "BeFree" (233733)

REAL TALK REFLECTION

1. What's something I used to think was "normal," but now realize could be illegal or unsafe?

....

....

2. Why is it hard for teens to know their rights when it comes to relationships or exploitation?

....

....

3. What would I say to a friend who thought they "deserved" what happened?

....

....

AFFIRMATION

I don't need a badge to know my worth.

I don't need bruises to name what's wrong.

I know the law, and I know I matter.

No one has the right to use me. Ever

CHAPTER 13: MORE RESOURCES & SAFE APPS

Where to Turn, Who to Text, and How to Get Help Fast

WHY THIS CHAPTER MATTERS

Sometimes you're not ready to talk. Sometimes you're afraid to say it out loud. And sometimes, you need help **right now**.

That's why this chapter exists.

To give you real tools, not just advice.

NATIONAL HOTLINES – 24/7, CONFIDENTIAL & FREE

Organization	Call or Text	What They Help With
National Human Trafficking Hotline	1-888-373-7888 or Text "BeFree" to 233733	Trafficking, grooming, suspicious online contact
Crisis Text Line	Text "HELLO" to 741741	Any emotional crisis, abuse, anxiety, grief, relationships
RAINN (Sexual Assault)	1-800-656-4673 or rainn.org	Sexual violence, support, and advocacy
National Runaway Safe-line	1-800-RUNAWAY	If you're unsafe at home or thinking about leaving
Trevor Project	Text "START" to 678678	LGBTQ+ youth in crisis or at risk
NCMEC CyberTipline	report.cybertip.org	Report online predators, CSAM, or grooming

APPS THAT HELP -- SAFELY

App	What It Does
My3	Crisis safety planning, who to call, where to go, what to say
Aspire News App	Disguised as a news app, but secretly lets you alert for help and document abuse
Circle of 6	Sends pre-written "come get me" messages to trusted friends
NotOK App	Tap a button to alert your safety circle in emergencies

Tip: Always install safety apps when calm and **hide or disguise them** if needed.

WHEN YOU FEEL STUCK

You can still ask for help even if:

- You don't know how to describe what's happening
- You don't want the person to "get in trouble"
- You're scared people won't believe you
- You made some choices you regret
- You've said no before and weren't heard

What's happening is still not your fault.

REAL TALK REFLECTION

1. Which hotline, app, or person feels like the most realistic option for me right now?

   ....

   ....

2. What's one thing I'd want someone to say to me in a moment of panic?

   ....

   ....

3. What could I screenshot, save, or write down today just in case I need it later?

   ....

   ....

AFFIRMATION

I may not have all the answers, but I am not helpless. I am not alone.
I have tools, I have options, and I have worth. Help is real.
Help is possible. And help is allowed.

CHAPTER 14: SELF-AFFIRMATION & HEALING JOURNAL

10 Prompts to Rebuild Confidence, Trust & Power

WHY JOURNALING?

Healing isn't just about surviving.

It's about reclaiming your voice, piece by piece. Journaling can help you:

- Name what happened without shame
- Process feelings that don't make sense
- Make space for hope, strength, and choice
- Say things you couldn't say out loud

No one has to read these pages but you. There's no "right" answer.

Just honesty.

PROMPT 1: "What I Wish Someone Had Said to Me"

What comfort, support, or truth do you wish someone had given you

....

....

....

PROMPT 2: "I'm Proud of Myself For…"

Even if it feels small, name the thing you survived or did anyway.

....

....

....

PROMPT 3: "What Makes Me Feel Safe Today?"

It could be a person, place, sound, or even a hoodie. Describe it.

....

....

....

PROMPT 4: "What Triggers Me and How I Want to Handle It"

Explore one thing that makes you feel anxious or scared. Then choose one gentle way to respond next time.

....

....

....

PROMPT 5: "My Boundaries Are Valid Because..."

Why do your limits matter, even if others don't respect them?

....

....

....

PROMPT 6: "A Memory I Need to Let Go Of"

Write it out. Rip it up later if needed. This is your release.

....

....

....

PROMPT 7: "The Kind of Love I Deserve"

What should real care, friendship, or love feel like?

....

....

....

PROMPT 8: "Who I'm Becoming"

Not what you've been through, but who you're growing into.

....

....

....

PROMPT 9: "What I Would Say to a Teen Going Through What I Did"

Be their safe voice. Be your own.

....

....

....

PROMPT 10: "Affirmations I Want to Believe, Even if It's Hard"

Try writing 3 truths you want to grow into.

1. ……………………………………………………………………..
2. ……………………………………………………………………..
3. ……………………………………………………………………

CLOSING AFFIRMATION

I am not what happened to me. I am who I choose to become.

This is not my ending, it's my rising.

CHAPTER 15: FINAL WORDS FROM THE AUTHOR

From My Heart to Yours

Dear Reader,

If you've made it this far, I want you to stop, breathe, and know something:

You are incredibly brave.

Whether you read this because you've been through something, know someone who has, or just wanted to understand the truth, your courage matters.

You've faced hard facts, ugly realities, and painful scenarios. And instead of shutting down, **you kept going**.

That says something powerful about you.

WHY I WROTE THIS BOOK

I didn't write this book just to "educate" you.

I wrote it because I've seen the gaps in schools, in conversations, in systems that are supposed to protect us.

I wrote it because I've sat across from teens who've said things like:

"I didn't know it was trafficking."

"He said it was love."

"I thought I couldn't tell anyone."

 "I thought it was my fault."

No more silence.

No more shame.

This book is my way of handing you a flashlight, something to help you or someone you care about find a way out of the dark.

You Are Not Alone

You may have been hurt.

You may still be healing.

You may have made decisions you regret.

But hear me clearly:

You are not what happened to you.

You are not broken.

You are not to blame.

You are worthy of safety.

You are allowed to speak.

You have every right to rise.

Keep Going

If you only remember one thing from this book, let it be this:

Predators win when you stay silent.

You win when you stay awake, aware, and unashamed.

Use your voice. Use your gut. Use your power.

And if the path feels hard, keep walking anyway. People are waiting to help you heal, protect your peace, and remind you how powerful you are.

I'm one of them.

With heart, truth, and hope,
Lisa N. Williams, MSW
Author • Advocate • Survivor Ally
LisaWms314@gmail.com
Safety & Respect Publishing
Motto: Empowering Pages… Empowering Young Minds One Page at a Time

GROUPS FOR SURVIVORS

Love is Respect: www.loveisrespect.org

Live peer chats, text & phone support for teens/young adults in dating abuse; safe space with trained advocates.

GEMS: www.gems-girls.org

Mentorship & life skills for girls (12–24) facing exploitation/trafficking; survivor-led leadership & healing.

Youth MOVE National: www.youthmovenational.org

Youth-led mental health, trauma, & justice support; local/online chapters with trauma-informed peer leaders.

The Lantern Project: www.ourrescue.org/lantern

Faith-based mentoring & community recovery for sex trafficking survivors.

StrongHearts Native Helpline: www.strongheartshelpline.org

Culturally-appropriate peer support for Native youth; call, chat, or text.

SafeBAE Student Ambassadors: www.safebae.org

Teen-led consent education, healing circles, & advocacy teams.

National Crittenton – Girl Talk: www.nationalcrittenton.org

Healing & leadership space for girls/gender-expansive youth impacted by trauma/justice system.

ONLINE PLATFORMS FOR PEER SUPPORT

7 Cups – www.7cups.com:
 Anonymous chat & teen-safe forums.

TrevorSpace – www.trevorspace.org:

LGBTQ+ youth community (13–24).

SAFETY APPS FOR TEENS & SURVIVORS

Aspire News: link, Disguised help app with emergency alerts.

Circle of 6: link, Quick alerts to 6 trusted contacts.

My Plan: link, Relationship safety planning.

Noonlight: www.noonlight.com, Panic button with GPS to 911.

SafeUT/Safe2Tell/Anonymous Alerts: School abuse/trafficking tip lines (varies by state).

bSafe: www.getbsafe.com: Live location, streaming, & fake call.

iAmDefendingMe: www.iamdefendingme.org: Auto-record & SOS alerts

LAW ENFORCEMENT & LEGAL SUPPORT

Nat'l Human Trafficking Hotline: 1-888-373-7888 **Text** BEFREE – link

FBI Human Trafficking Unit –link

Local/State Police: Request SVU or Trafficking Task Force.

DHS Blue Campaign: link Report: 1-866-347-2423

Legal Aid: Human Trafficking Legal Center – www.htlegalcenter.org

CAST: www.castla.org

Victim Rights Law Center: www.victimrights.org

Break the Cycle; www.breakthecycle.org: Teen legal advocacy.

Nat'l Crime Victim Bar Assoc: www.victimbar.org

MY SAFETY PLAN

- Safe adults I can call if I need help:

- Places I feel safe:

- My emergency code word is:

- Local emergency numbers:

- Warning signs, I will watch for:

QUICK SAFETY CHECKLIST

STAYING SAFE ONLINE & IN REAL LIFE

1. Trust Your Instincts: If something feels wrong, it probably is.

2. Limit Personal Info: Don't share your full name, school, or location online.

3. Privacy Settings: Keep your social media private and limit who can contact you.

4. Be Cautious with Photos: Never send revealing pictures, even to people you trust.

5. Meet New People Safely: Always meet in a public place with someone you trust.

6. Keep Your Phone Charged: Have emergency contacts saved.

7. Create a Safety Word: A code you can use with family/friends to signal danger.

8. Know Escape Routes: Be aware of exits in any place you visit.

9. Have a Trusted Circle: Identify 3–5 trusted adults you can contact anytime.

10. Set Boundaries: Say no to anything that makes you uncomfortable.

11. Use the Buddy System: Don't Walk alone at night or in unfamiliar areas.

12. Know Public Resources: Memorize local safe places (police, shelters, libraries).

13. Trustworthy Transportation: Use verified rideshare apps or share your ride details.

14. Keep Your ID Safe: Carry an ID and emergency contacts.

15. Stay Alert: Avoid distractions like loud music or texting while walking.

16. Speak Up: If a friend seems at risk, get help even if it feels awkward.

17. Memorize Helplines: National Human Trafficking Hotline: **1-888-373-7888.**

18. Plan for Emergencies: Know who to call, where to go, and what to do.

About the Author

Lisa N. Williams, MSW is a therapist, trauma specialist, child advocate, and fierce believer in the power of informed youth.

With over three decades of experience across child protection, juvenile justice, and clinical support services, Lisa has worked with at-risk youth and families as a voice of compassion and truth. She holds a Master of Social Work (MSW) from Washington University in St. Louis and a Bachelors in Criminal Justice from Lincoln University Jefferson City, Missouri.

She has served in frontline roles with the **Missouri Division of Youth Services**, **Missouri Division of Family Services**, and the **Illinois Department of Children and Family Services**, and currently supports fathers as a trauma specialist/ therapist at **Fathers & Families Support Center**.

Lisa brings a rare blend of professional insight and real-world heart to every page she writes. Her work empowers teens with facts, language, and tools to outsmart predators, trust their instincts, and reclaim their power.

She is the founder of **Safety & Respect Publishing**, which delivers trauma-informed, culturally aware resources for youth, families, schools, and community programs nationwide.

Want to bring Lisa to your school, youth center, or conference? Whether it's a classroom discussion, a parent workshop, or a professional training, Lisa brings:

- Truth without shame
- Tools without overwhelm
- Trauma-informed expertise
- Real stories that connect

Contact:

LisaWms314@gmail.com

Based in Missouri, available nationally

Leave a Review

If this book helped you, your teen, your students, or someone you care about…

Please take 2 minutes to leave a review on Amazon.

Your review helps this book reach:

- More teens in danger
- More schools and libraries
- More parents who need support
- More communities ready to make a change

Search the title:

"What Human Traffickers Don't Want You to Know: A Teen's Guide to Outsmarting Predators"

Your words could help someone decide to take the book home and take their safety back.

Back Cover Elements

Tagline (top):

Outsmart the lies. Own your voice. Stay safe.

Book Description: WHAT HUMAN TRAFFICKERS DON'T WANT YOU TO KNOW: A TEENS GUIDE TO OUTSMARTING THE PREDATOR is a bold, honest, and empowering guide that arms teens with the truth about grooming, exploitation, and manipulation. Written by trauma specialist and advocate Lisa N. Williams, MSW, this book speaks directly to 8th–12th grade readers using real-life case files, safety tools, reflection prompts, and survivor wisdom.

Whether read in classrooms or at home, it gives youth what predators fear most: **knowledge, language, and power.**

Features Include:

- Fear Factor boxes for truth-based awareness
- Mini case studies and real-world scenarios
- Grooming red flags and online safety checklists
- Trauma-informed, secular, and inclusive language
- Self-affirmation journal and recovery tools

Endorsements:

"This guide gives teens the tools they need to recognize red flags and protect themselves. It's empowering, honest, and exactly what families need right now."

Porchia W., Parent/Advocate

"As someone who has overseen countless child protection investigations, I can confidently say this book fills a critical gap."

Shelly S., Retired Child Investigation Administrator

"This should be required reading in every middle and high school. I appreciate the trauma-informed approach."

Fern B., Licensed Clinical Social Worker

"I've seen firsthand how traffickers manipulate vulnerable youth—this book speaks their language before the streets do. It's not just informative, it's preventative. Every teen should read it."

Bri'on S., Juvenile Corrections Officer

Author Bio: Lisa N. Williams, MSW is a trauma therapist and child advocate with over 30 years of experience in youth protection and social work. She is the founder of Safety & Respect Publishing, dedicated to creating empowering, trauma-informed resources for youth and families. Lisa brings real-world experience, professional training, and deep heart to every page.

Barcode Area: Bottom right (leave 2"x1.2" clear zone)

- **Back cover above barcode**
- **Optional small version on spine**

www.ingramcontent.com/pod-product-compliance
Lightning Source LLC
Chambersburg PA
CBHW070816280326
41934CB00012B/3196